SPIRIT

PARENTING

Healing brokenness in the Family Structure

By: LaTonya Page~Balkcom

SPIRIT LED APPROACH
TO
PARENTING

Healing brokenness in the Family Structure

WRITTEN BY:
LATONYA PAGE ~ BALKCOM

SPIRIT LED APPROACH TO PARENTING
Healing brokenness in the Family Structure

My suggestions are consciously practical. For those of you who have been seeking practical suggestions on how to empower or relate to some of the most unique live, African American children, this book will help with what comes from, common sense and wisdom from biblical scriptures and revelations from our Ancient Ancestors guiding common sense. I hope that it gives help to those who are attempting to parent without a complete family unit and does not mind parenting with help from the guidance of a higher power, the creator of all men, women and children.

With over thirty years of parenting, I have learned how spirituality and parenting goes hand and hand. No matter how great your love is for your child, they will always find a way to show you, how imperfect you are. Likewise, you will begin to see how imperfect your little angels are no matter how great your compassion and love is, your patience will be tested.

SPIRIT LED APPROACH TO PARENTING
Healing brokenness in the Family Structure

But thank God for the hope that lies in the heart of every Spiritual family that these children will come to know their African Culture and African Spirituality and will go on to live full prosperous lives.

Part one
National responsibilities
SPIRIT LED APPROACH TO PARENTING
Healing brokenness in the Family Structure

SPIRIT LED APPROACH TO PARENTING
Healing brokenness in the Family Structure

Sad as it may sound. Many families today have no sense of continuity or regard for spirituality being the foundation of raising a family. Nor are they aware of the blessings attached to knowing about Higher Power. (Psalm. 33:12, KJV)

Yes, parenting is work. It requires time, patience and effort showered with plenty of love and understanding. It is not selfish or selfless. It is hard soul-labor. It requires you to rise to all occasions, constantly praying, and devotion of twenty-five hours a day.

Parenting requires, gentleness, temperance and longsuffering and faith. (Galatians 5:22, KJV)

I know the idea of a success story may seem unreal and not attainable especially when you are dealing with African American teenagers who have been targeted by the system their whole life. Many have been diagnosed with behavioral disorders.

They have developed that system mentality where no matter what you say to them, nothing seems to matter much because they do not trust anyone.
You see great potential and desire to empower them to believe that they can achieve whatever they put their minds to.

However, the only things they want to do are, disrespect all authority figures. The more the merrier. You advocate putting them in the best schools, only to be informed, that they are cutting classes and cursing the teachers out, fighting, doing drugs with peers on a daily basis.

SPIRIT LED APPROACH TO PARENTING
Healing brokenness in the Family Structure

Although you provide for them three meals a day, breakfast lunch and dinner, they skip meals.
No matter how you buy them the best of clothing; they rip them up or loan them out and even lose them.

You put them in after school activities to broaden their horizons. They do not want to go. You spend countless hours laboring and talking to them about the importance of polishing social skills and correcting their behaviors but, still you get cussed out and oftentimes, they lie to the Social worker or Case manager at school, just so that they can be taken out of your home and placed into a foster home. Why? Because this is what they have become accustom to doing to get their way.

Despite your efforts to make them feel safe, loved, unique, secure, accepted, respected, and appreciated, it still does not matter to them.

SPIRIT LED APPROACH TO PARENTING
Healing brokenness in the Family Structure

You wake up one day and they have stolen your wallet and have set the house on fire while you are in it. Yes, I still say,

Healing brokenness in the African American Family Structure

We as African American parents have a national responsibility to help save the lives of these unique children.

In the midst all these situations, we are more than conquerors and will gain a surpassing victory if we do not faint and fell.

Part Two
Love

Love
SPIRIT LED APPROACH TO PARENTING
Healing brokenness in the Family Structure

As the father hath loved me, so have I loved you.
If ye keep my commandments, ye shall abide in my
love; even as I have kept my Father's
commandments, and abide in his love.
These things have I spoken unto you, that my joy
might remain in you, and that your joy might be
full.
This is my commandment, that ye love one
another, as I have loved you.
Greater love hath no man than this that a man lay
down his life for his friends. (John 15:9-13 KJV)

Love cultivates, enriches, and promotes
wholeness. These unique lives need enormous
amounts of reassurance and love. Children of
this particular genre are often starving for love
and usually resort to negative behaviors,
assuming that this will lead to receiving love
from parents and teachers.

Oftentimes an unhealthy self-regard or improper
self- focus is the cause, and is   rooted from their
biological parents, parents…parents. That's
right. This thing extends all the

way back to slavery. Many of their personalities has become tainted by rejection. We as African American parents need to realize that the destiny of their soul may rest upon us.

Therefore, we must love these unique children without assaulting their character farther or instilling despair. We must do this by understanding the practical *application of the* word of god about love. Teaching these unique children, that god loves them regardless of their deficiencies, generously.

Giving honest praise and a lot of it along with clear understanding about who God is and why God loves them so much will develop proper self-image.

Many of these unique children hold fears in their hearts, which is a clear sign that they may lack the knowledge of how much God loves them. Once they come into the knowledge of God's love, the fear will fade away.

It is difficult for them to believe that God loves them because all they have seen are the overwhelming pressure, which comes along with being an African American child or teen. This is why it is so important for us as African American parents to assure them that God knows everything about them. He knows their every thought. He knows where they have rested their heads every moment of their lives. They can never be lost in God. They are precious to the lord. Reminding them to remember he is thinking of them at all times.

Love
SPIRIT LED APPROACH TO PARENTING
Healing brokenness in the Family Structure

"and therefore the lord waits(expecting, looking and longing) to be gracious to you; and therefore He lifts himself up, that He may have mercy on you and show loving-kindness to you. For the lord is a God of justice. Blessed (happy, fortunate) are all those who wait for him, who expect and look and long for him (for his love, his peace, his joy, his victory, unbroken relationship)!" (Isaiah 30:18).

Let us encourage our unique children to experience the love of a Higher Power. Reminding them that no matter what happens, God's love is everlasting. He is able to free them from all their fears and feelings of rejection. God guards and rescues all who love and give him praise. Encourage them to confess daily, repeatedly, "God loves me." His love is abundant and assuring.

Part Three
Guidance
SPIRIT LED APPROACH TO PARENTING
Healing brokenness in the Family Structure

SPIRIT LED APPROACH TO PARENTING
Healing brokenness in the Family Structure

Many of our unique African American children come into our schools with little to no guidance or structure in their lives. Most of them have a poor sense of self, with limited living skills and not to mention, lack of morals and values.

Simple things like washing their hands after they use the toilet, sounds foreign to them. Saying things like, "please and thank you", do not come natural. Respecting adults and or other people's property has not been apart of their everyday living. Taking baths, brushing their teeth was never routine. Daily routines like, attending school on a regular basis, seems unimportant.

However, they would rather be, left alone to be whatever they have become, rather than become introduced to something new and different that would enrich there lives. As parents and Educators, to these unique individuals are often not prepared for the task of teaching these youngsters, in many cases, at such a late age, to become more self-aware.

SPIRIT LED APPROACH TO PARENTING
Healing brokenness in the Family Structure

One may wonder if the teaching will even accomplish anything. Absolutely, we must pay close attention to continue to believe in these children natural and spiritual potentials.

For example, there was a foster child teenager in my home. One morning while I was drinking my morning cup of coffee at the kitchen table, she came down stairs in her bathrobe and proceeded to open the back door to step outside.

SPIRIT LED APPROACH TO PARENTING
Healing brokenness in the Family Structure

I thought it strange that she would be going outside in her bathrobe, so I quickly ran up the steps to my bedroom to see where she was going so early in the morning, not even dressed. She could not see that I was peaking out of my bedroom window at her, as she grabbed a plastic bag filled with cannabis. That is right!

She arrived back at the door with her big round eyes looking surprised that I was standing, blocking her from entering my home. "Where are you going with those drugs?" Her eyes widened with guilt. In her silence came the scent of what she can only liken to marijuana, a smell apparently she thought I was unaware of. With avoidance in her eyes, she responded, "mom, this is not mine, I am holding it for someone."

With a firm voice, I told her to, "get those drugs away from my house, and don't ever let me catch her stashing drugs in my backyard ever again. What you have done is wrong!" She responded, "It's not wrong. It's only wrong if I get caught."

SPIRIT LED APPROACH TO PARENTING
Healing brokenness in the Family Structure

My mind reflected back... *This girl was practically raised in the system. She has been in several homes. She has heard numerous conversations from me that touched on spiritual things and especially on personal ethics like staying away from trouble (preschool and primary style, of course). In addition, she actually thinks that holding drugs is ok, as long as you don't get caught.*

These unique individuals can easily succumb to delusion in their thinking, as you can see. However, foster parents must intercede with prayer and spiritual and parental guidance if we hope to enhance these children's development. We must lead by example.

SPIRIT LED APPROACH TO PARENTING
Healing brokenness in theFamily Structure

Sensitivity morally does not come to these unique minds easily. Many of them are not even aware of their capacity for good and evil, an acquaintance that began in early childhood years.

With a common sense approach, help them to understand that innately, they are equipped with an moral compass or barometer. Resist the parental impulse to lecture, but with consistent eye contact, listen. Try to follow what they are saying although it may seem illogical then explain what you believe and why. They will appreciate you and eventually themselves despite their inadequacies or mistakes.

This will help cultivate them to work at their development.

SPIRIT LED APPROACH TO PARENTING
Healing brokenness in theFamily Structure

Prayer is the place to begin. Effective communication and communicating spiritual qualities to these unique children and allowing them the space to grow will appeal to their conscience and enable us to see that our efforts and motivation must be nothing less than to give all the glory to God.

(1 Corinthians. 10:31 Whether therefore ye eat, or drink, or whatsoever ye do, do all to the glory of God:)

Part four
Help and care
SPIRIT LED APPROACH TO PARENTING
Healing brokenness in the Family Structure

Help and care
SPIRIT LED APPROACH TO PARENTING
Healing brokenness in the Family Structure

Common sense tells us that any effective parenting must consist of the ability to help and care for these unique individuals lives. Candidly, this is not something you just devote spare time to, or do it if you like. This requires hard soul-labor.

None of us can make up for the missed time in these children lives. However, we can remedy some of the problems with ongoing encouragement and guidance amidst the recurrent doubts that come to them, along with fears and uncertainty of never being stable and never having anyone to care nor help them in their time of need.

Children can sense, when they are not regarded as people and are not taken seriously, especially teenagers. When they come to live in your home, they can be coarse. Shouting obscenities, urinating on the front lawn, in broad daylight, extremely untidy, playing loud music all day and nights, playing with matches, writing on the beds and walls with markers and the list goes on.

Help and care
<u>SPIRIT LED APPROACH TO PARENTING</u>
Healing brokenness in the Family Structure

During these unpleasant times, we may find ourselves feeling disgusted, while seeing no good in them. Dealing with these unique lives, we must show kindness through times such as these. *"(Colossians 3:14)And above all these things put on charity (love), which is the perfect bond of perfect ness (unity)"*

Being distraught and furious will only lead to bitterness.

<u>SPIRIT LED APPROACH TO PARENTING</u>
Healing brokenness in the Family Structure

We must find a common sense approach to reaching these unique individuals, an approach that will manifest itself in profound love.

Many of these unique lives display rude behaviors because of feelings of helplessness. They are impatient and demanding and are without self-control.

Once there was a young boy, who after being outside in the snow playing one day, decided to come in and walk on my newly installed white carpet with his slushy boots. I repeatedly asked him to wait by the door, until I found a rug for him to place his shoes on, of course, he ignored me.

My first instinct was to yell and scream at him. Instead, I decided to pursue my journey to find a rug. After I found the rug, I called the little boy back downstairs. I gave him a towel to wipe up his mess and redirected him towards his boots that he had thrown in the middle of his bedrooms floor.

Help and care
SPIRIT LED APPROACH TO PARENTING
Healing brokenness in the Family Structure

I instructed him in a firm voice, to pick them up and to place the boots on the rug at the door and reminded him to remove his boots before going upstairs. I also reminded him that expects him to listen to me when I am speaking to him.

We cannot be afraid to impose obvious limitations on these children. Having healthy boundaries and respect toward each other will better the communication. We do more harm than good if we ignore children with bad behavior. Set healthy boundaries.

Parents must become advocates of discipline, non-corporal demonstrated through love.

Part five
Fear
SPIRIT LED APPROACH TO PARENTING
Healing brokenness in the Family Structure

SPIRIT LED APPROACH TO PARENTING
Healing brokenness in the Family Structure

Unwavering fears have ultimately dominated the lives of these unique African American individuals. With their parents either giving them up or losing them through the courts, oftentimes because of neglect or many forms of abuse, has left them feeling abandoned and without support. They are terrified and filled with dread. Many of them have gone through a life of difficulty, which has left them feeling oppressed. Frightened, timid, and afraid are the emotions that ripple through the hearts of these children.

This is why as parents we must deliver little by little, spiritual passages, from Biblical text, that will ultimately completely deliver them from this false evidence appearing real.

Many of these children cannot see pass their present situation. Negative thinking habits or patterns have taken over their senses. We know that this is just the enemy telling them that their current situation will never change and their future will be failure.

SPIRIT LED APPROACH TO PARENTING
Healing brokenness in Family Structure

We must help them to declare the word of God over their lives. We must teach them to confess scriptures on fear, aloud, establishing in the spiritual realm that they do not intend to live in fear.

Memorize these verses below and repeat them every time they are tempted to become anxious and fearful.

"For god hath not given us the spirit of fear; (timidity, cowardice) but of power, and of love, and of a sound (calm and well-balanced) mind. (2 timothy 1:7) KJV

"Fear thou not; for I am with thee; be not dismayed; for I am thy God; I will strengthen thee; yea, I will help thee; I will uphold thee with the right hand of my righteousness". (Isaiah 41:10) KJV

<u>Part six</u>
Disappointment, Anxiety, and Worry
<u>SPIRIT LED APPROACH TO PARENTING</u>
Healing brokenness in the Family Structure

Disappointment, anxiety, and worry
SPIRIT LED APPROACH TO PARENTING
Healing brokenness in the Family Structure

Common sense tells us that these unique African American individuals have suffered through major disappointments in their lives that have produced anxieties and worries alike.

Many of their lives were compromised, by being born into a family with one parent. Often that abused drugs or alcohol. Oftentimes being physically and sexually abused them. Perhaps, the vulnerability became reinforced, when placed in the foster system because of their parents neglect, ultimately leaving them feeling abandoned.

Many of them experienced one or both parents drunken rages and or weekly binges that left them worried whether or not they would see their parents again, where the next meal would come from and or anxiety over knowing they were going to be beaten again, once their parent finished drinking or drugging.

Disappointment, anxiety, and worry
SPIRIT LED APPROACH TO PARENTING
Healing brokenness in the Family Structure

Some of them had to become the parent at the age of six if they had siblings. Taking this position often leaves them feeling the need to survive the onslaught of the parent's alcoholism or drug abuse, plaguing them with feelings of self-doubt.

Perhaps because they had to learn to find answers and solutions that are really beyond their level of maturity. Many of them are unlearned in skills that will provide life-long age-appropriate functions. They end up living with ongoing sense of inadequacy, insecurity, and failures.

Many times, I have witnessed how these children feel the need to keep the conflicts hidden deep inside appearing self-sufficient however possesses a profound desire to be guided and cared for unconditionally.

Disappointment, anxiety, and worry
<u>**SPIRIT LED APPROACH TO PARENTING**</u>
Healing brokenness in the Family Structure

Perhaps their lack of awareness of their deeper issues prevents them from ever resolving these conflicts.

Many African American children and teens are tormented, with feelings they cannot acknowledge or relinquish. Often time's bad behavior plays out these feelings over and over again. Many of their realities inward and outward become threats that they must defend against rather than riches to be sought after and enjoyed.

Unhappy with their life and wanting to change, but are unable to because of the repeat self-destructive behaviors, emotionally they blame circumstances or others for what they do. Remaining the victim, they are become trapped in the helpless little person mentality.

Disappointment, anxiety, and worry
SPIRIT LED APPROACH TO PARENTING
Healing brokenness in the Family Structure

This is why we as extensions of our Ancestors must use a spiritual approach to helping these unique lives understand the importance of knowing who they are culturally and Spiritually... as their mother and father.

(Philippians 3:13-14) Brethren, I count not myself to have apprehended; but this one thing I do, forgetting those things, which are behind, and reaching forth unto those things, which are before. I press toward the mark for the prize of the high calling of God in Christ Jesus". **KJV**

Teaching them to find comfort in A Power greater than themselves during the conflict perhaps should be one of the first life lessons any should learn.

SPIRIT LED APPROACH TO PARENTING
Healing brokenness in the Family Structure

(Isaiah 43:18-19) Remember ye not the former things, neither consider the things of the old. Behold, I will do a new thing; now it shall spring forth; shall ye not know it? I will even make a way in the wilderness and rivers in the desert". KJV

Teach them that yet in the midst of all adversities, they are more than a conqueror and will be victorious through believing in themselves, the Ancestors that came before them and the Creator of All.

Part seven
Comfort
SPIRIT LED APPROACH TO PARENTING
Healing brokenness in the Family Structure

SPIRIT LED APPROACH TO PARENTING
Healing brokenness in the Family Structure

Perhaps, all African American children can be viewed as wounded individuals. They are hurting in places the human eye cannot see. Their pain is worst than you or I could ever imagine. This is why we need spiritual intervention in the lives of these unique individuals. The healing power and the anointed touch of God, is the only one who can reach the places these children who have been all, but assassinated.

Restoration is, desperately needed in the lives of each child placed in our homes. The enemy wanted to destroy their lives but God and the Ancestors wants to change their destiny. Putting back the pieces in these children's lives is by far something we mere humans can do by ourselves. Divine intervention is the only way.

Perhaps, we as African American parents, were divinely created to help these children meet there visions.

SPIRIT LED APPROACH TO PARENTING
Healing brokenness in the Family Structure

We must encourage and exhort this children to continue to grow to move forward until the pains of their past becomes less important or forgotten. We must continue to comfort, motivate, and nurture them through the pain until newness fills them within.

Compassion produces a lasting change. Without it, there will be no healing.

Just as the disciples thought, they would die when the storm had troubled the waters. They challenged Christ compassion. They went to the back of the ship and said, "(Carest thou not that we perish?" Mark 4:38).

SPIRIT LED APPROACH TO PARENTING
Healing brokenness in the Family Structure

These unique lives need us to come to their aid, by way of prayer. They have imprisoned themselves with fears.

Just as the story of Jesus rebuking that storm in the good book of stories, So should we rebuke the storm that torments these unique African American lives "(Peace, be still". Mark 4:39)

Part eight
Self-Image
SPIRIT LED APPROACH TO PARENTING
Healing brokenness in the Family Structure

Self-Image
SPIRIT LED APPROACH TO PARENTING
Healing brokenness in the Family Structure

Many of these unique lives are packaged with insecurities, vulnerabilities, and fears. Their eye tells the story along with their posture. Perhaps, their self-esteem is at the lowest when they come into the system.

Every time I would see a young African American teenage girl with her skirt barely covering her behind or wearing a pair of stilettos that screams, streetwalker, I see some form of child abuse looking me right in the face. Low self-esteem is not prejudice. Males and females can experience all levels of low self-image, coupled with fear.

These children have learned to camouflage their fears, which are tragic enough to destroy their self-image. They learn to bury them deep inside by using alcohol and drugs and by indulging in sex at a very early age.

Working with young women and men who were addicted to drugs and alcohol has taught me that perhaps an addiction knows no age limit. In addition, young girls contracting the HIV virus by the age of twelve perhaps enlightened me of how broken these unique individuals really are. They have become prisoners of Spiritual Warfare. Perhaps, many of these children have the potential to become successful lives if only they were not carrying this secret pain. The bible tells the story of those who have fallen prey to the snares of Satan.

"Mark: 10-16 And they brought young children to him, that he should touch them: and his disciples rebuked those that brought them.

SPIRIT LED APPROACH TO PARENTING
Healing brokenness in the Family Structure

Cont':But when Jesus saw it, he was much displeased, and said unto them, Suffer the little children to come unto me, and forbid them not: for of such is the kingdom of God. Verily I say unto you, whosoever shall not receive the kingdom of God as a little child, he shall not enter therein. And he took them up in his arms, put his hands upon them, and blessed them.)" KJV

Many of these unique individuals come from broken homes and most become confused by the brokenness of the family unit.

Perhaps, we must possess the insight and the divine wisdom of the Ancestors to heal these unique individual lives. This is what it will take.

Part nine
Growing spiritually
SPIRIT LED APPROACH TO PARENTING
Healing brokenness in the Family Structure

SPIRIT LED APPROACH TO PARENTING
Healing brokenness in the Family Structure

We must touch the lives of these unique individuals with encouragement and the word of hope, which is the word of God and the Ancestors. These children are the future.

We must encourage these children to rest in a relationship with the highest God. Even in the promises of God. There is a sense of security in having a relationship with A Higher Power.

Girls more than boys, tend to have a need for stability. They possess the need to be more nurtured and protected. This is what originally Adam role was towards Eve.

Perhaps, understanding the possibilities linked with knowing African culture and a higher Power and understand the promises made in regards to covering or protecting the uncovered or unprotected is fundamental. God will not allow you to spend the rest of your life feeling violated or exposed.

Growing spiritually
SPIRIT LED APPROACH TO PARENTING
Healing brokenness in the Family Structure

Many of these children are violated emotionally early in life. Perhaps leaving them mentally vulnerable, to corrupt imaginations. This is why it is important to reach out and embrace these young lives, allowing God through you, to heal their scars by sharing the word of God and speaking the word of God over their lives.

To know your own Culture and Spirituality is important in every child's life.

SPIRIT LED APPROACH TO PARENTING
Healing brokenness in the Family Structure

The mind and the emotions needs constant reassuring and consolation, and only God can provide these unique African American individuals with the assurance and security needed to live a life that was once, seemingly overwhelming, full of uncertainties and relentless fear.

We must be determined to find the treasures in each one of these unique individuals' lives that was at one time, disregarded, and pray for complete restoration and a willingness of the heart to receive the process of reconstruction by A Higher Power and the Ancestors guidance.

Growing spiritually
SPIRIT LED APPROACH TO PARENTING
Healing brokenness in the Family Structure

"(Hebrews 6:17-18 because God wanted to make the unchanging nature of his purpose very clear to the heirs of what was promised, he confirmed it with an oath. God did this so that, by two unchangeable things in which it is impossible for God to lie, we who have fled to take hold of the hope offered to us may be greatly encouraged.") *[NIv]*
It is beneficial to have a relationship with a Higher Power and to daily practice Spiritual ethics and even memorizing the 42 Laws of Maat. The payoff is a victorious life.

42 Laws of Maat

1. I HONOR VIRTUE
2. I BENEFIT WITH GRATITUDE
3. I AM PEACEFUL
4. I RESPECT THE PROPERTY OF OTHERS
5. I GIVE OFFERINGS THAT ARE GENUINE
6. I AFFIRM THAT ALL LIFE IS SACRED
7. I LIVE IN TRUTH
8. I REGARD ALL ALTARS WITH RESPECT
9. I SPEAK WITH SINCERITY
10. I CONSUME ONLY MY FAIR SHARE
11. I OFFER WORDS OF GOOD INTENT
12. I RELATE IN PEACE
13. I HONOR ANIMALS WITH REVERENCE
14. I CAN BE TRUSTED
15. I CARE FOR THE EARTH
16. I KEEP MY OWN COUNCIL
17. I SPEAK POSITIVELY OF OTHERS
18. I REMAIN IN BALANCE WITH MY EMOTIONS
19. I AM TRUSTFUL IN MY RELATIONSHIPS
20. I HOLD PURITY IN HIGH ESTEEM
21. I SPREAD JOY
22. I DO THE BEST I CAN
23. I COMMUNICATE WITH COMPASSION
24. I LISTEN TO OPPOSING OPINION
25. I CREATE HARMONY
26. I INVOKE LAUGHTER

27. I AM OPEN TO LOVE IN VARIOUS FORMS
28. I AM FORGIVING
29. I AM KIND
30. I AM RESPECTFUL OF OTHERS
31. I AM ACCEPTING
32. I FOLLOW MY INNER GUIDANCE
33. I CONVERSE WITH AWARENESS
34. I DO GOOD
35. I GIVE BLESSINGS
36. I KEEP THE WATERS PURE
37. I SPEAK WITH GOOD INTENT
38. I PRAISE THE GODDESS AND THE GOD
39. I AM HUMBLE
40. I ACHIEVE WITH INTEGRITY
41. I ADVANCE THROUGH MY OWN ABILITIES
42. I EMBRACE THE ALL

42 Laws of Maat

Part Ten
Victorious
SPIRIT LED APPROACH TO PARENTING
Healing brokenness in the Family Structure

If you are an African American parent and have had the privilege to birth and experienced working with one or more of these hurting, and unique individuals, I salute you.

If you are the one who has prayed one of these unique lives through, than know that the call on your life is high.

Through the strange interruptions of discourse that busied your days. God blessed you through the stress.

When they mean mugged you, you hugged them.

Though they would insult you and assaulted you, a smile came through.

Instead of agonizing over their problems, you prayed and strategically found the solution.

Victorious
SPIRIT LED APPROACH TO PARENTING
Healing brokenness in the Family Structure

When they would not tolerate you, you celebrated them.

When they displayed acts of hatred, you showed mounds of faith.

When they acted despondent, your Love responded.

David said, "(Psalm 27:13 I had fainted, unless I had believed to see the goodness of the lord in the land of the living").

Perhaps, many of us seeing through a natural eye, would never expect these unique individuals to change. Because, when many of them come into our homes, they appear unreachable.

SPIRIT LED APPROACH TO PARENTING
Healing brokenness in the Family Structure

"(Proverbs 29:18Where there is no vision, the people perish".)

Perhaps, this is why we must possess the faith to see change for them. They cannot envision a change for their lives if they cannot see it for themselves. Their brokenness weakens them from tearing themselves loose from their past pain, hindering them from moving forward in the healing process by faith.

"(Hebrews 11:6 But without faith it is impossible to please him: for he that cometh to God must believe that he is, and that he is a rewarder of them that diligently seek him.")

We must believe that God is powerful enough to destroy the bondages of the enemy in their life. God will set them free. We must plant God's seed of truth in the lives of these children. No matter how hard the task, we as foster parents must work to nourish the minds, and encourage the hearts of these children.

The biblical scripture reminds us:
SPIRIT LED APPROACH TO PARENTING
Healing brokenness in the Family Structure

"I will praise thee; for I am fearfully and wonderfully made: marvelous are thy works; and that my soul knoweth right well."
(Psalms 139:12)

"I can do all things through Christ which strengtheneth me." (Philippians 4:13)

"And the Lord shall make thee the head, and not the tail; and thou shalt be above only, and thou shalt not be beneath". (Deuteronomy 28:13)

Although the enemy viciously attacks their lives, God is able to make their lives victorious.

The biblical scripture reminds us:
SPIRIT LED APPROACH TO PARENTING
Healing brokenness in the Family Structure

All God needs is an opportunity to work in the lives of these unique individuals. You and I can supply this great opportunity by tuning in to the unadulterated words of God and speaking the word of God into the lives of the less fortunate.

Do not allow the circumstances of these children's past to dictate their futures. Past hurts and pains designed by the enemy to keep them from reaching their fullest potential. Help them to see the beauty of all the different stages in their lives that ultimately led them to know A Higher Power and the Guidance of our Ancestors.

The victory is that God kept them throughout their struggles.

SPIRIT LED APPROACH TO PARENTING

Healing brokenness in the Family Structure

LaTonya Page-Balkcom
Dedication

*I dedicate this book to the memory of my Mother,
the late Evangelist. Ernestine Jones~Page,
whose unfailing love for God, her husband
and children, defined my sense of
motherhood and has provided me, my first
opportunity to encounter teachings of The
Most High and my Ancestors guidance,
that gave me a Mind of Excellence and
Perseverance and Determination.
To My father
Herman Page Sr.
To my children:*

*Iiesha Ernestine, Natalie Joy Balkcom
Also to my grand children,
Mia Simone, Prince Martin William, Ivy Latonia
For without all of you, there would be no book*

SPIRIT LED APPROACH
TO
PARENTING

Healing brokenness in the Family Structure

LaTonya Page-Balkcom
Dedication

Finally,

To my friend Sheldon Bailey of New Orleans, who believed in me and my ability to write a book.

SPIRIT LED APPROACH TO PARENTING

Healing brokenness in the Family Structure

About the book

Spirit led approach to parenting is from the heart of a women who not only dedicated her life to her own child and grandchildren …but also dedicated her life to helping physically and mentally abused, sexually abuse and medically complexes foster children for many years.

Every African American Parent and Foster parent in this country who reads this book, through faith in a Higher Power and/or knowledge of Maat 42 Laws, Christianity or African cultures, can ultimately influence the lives of these unique children and help transform the lives, minds, and spirits of African American children and foster children or any nationality…through the simple teachings of the Laws of Maat, African Spirituality, Biblical teachings along with Guidance of our Ancestors..And our Higher Power. The Creator of All things. A'se

Contents
SPIRIT LED APPROACH
TO
PARENTING

Healing brokenness in the Family Structure

Contents
SPIRIT LED APPROACH
TO
PARENTING

Healing brokenness in the Family Structure

SPIRIT LED APPROACH TO PARENTING

Healing brokenness in the Family Structure

SPIRIT LED APPROACH
TO
PARENTING

Healing brokenness in the Family Structure

SPIRIT LED APPROACH
TO
PARENTING

Healing brokenness in the Family Structure

Part 10: Victorious

SPIRIT LED APPROACH TO PARENTING

Healing brokenness in the Family Structure

I became a foster care provider. My first foster child left indelibly engraved footprints across my memory for many reasons. I believe that my life was in some cosmic way, spiritually drawn into Joy's life and direction. Indeed, this was a divine connection.

Perhaps the most memorable event of our acquaintance as I will never forget is when the Department of Children and Family Services removed this child I had adopted, my little angel Joy, from my home.

Joy was a bright eyed, loving baby, with medical complexes that only I was ordained by the Most High to nurture. I would watch in amazement for seven long years,

SPIRIT LED APPROACH
TO
PARENTING

Healing brokenness in the Family Structure

as I cultivated Joy's little mind into learning until she had reached beyond ever known milestone that was placed on her life by her Doctors.

Embedded in my consciousness was the Will to do, exceedingly above all that was required of me that would ultimately give Joy the Will and Courage to Thrive, after being labeled, "Failure to Thrive". In my eyes, only I housed the stamina and resilience it took to care for such a child.

As CeCe Winans sings in one of her songs titled "Alabaster Box", "No one knows the cost of the oil in my Alabaster box!"

SPIRIT LED APPROACH
TO
PARENTING

Healing brokenness in the Family Structure

It costs much more than I had ever imagined being a foster caregiver.

While living in another part of Illinois for only a month, my doorbell rang.
The woman was from the Department of Children and Family Services who entered into my home and removed Joy from my care behind false allegations of abuse from another foster child and the unscrupulous act of deception from my biological daughter's boyfriend at the time.

The other foster child received a suspension from school and decided to shift the attention off herself onto me, by falsifying allegations of abuse.

SPIRIT LED APPROACH TO PARENTING

Healing brokenness in the Family Structure

What happened next? I became homeless and indigent in a matter of hours. The hurt and pain I endured year after year, behind losing Joy, ultimately caused my Heart to beat irregularly and I ended up on Heart medication with my heart operating at 55%.

I believe that in order to truly be fully successful at parenting, foster parents must be given legal protection against being falsely accused of abuse by savvy teenagers and children alike who have become systemized and know how to play the system against their placement at random.

SPIRIT LED APPROACH
TO
PARENTING

Healing brokenness in the Family Structure

Perhaps, it is the cumulative efforts of State Agencies and The Juvenile Court system to provide hope, healing, and help for everyone involved, for both foster child and the foster parent. Perhaps this would lower the statistics of failed placement and adoptions as a whole.

We are not interested in mere placement of a child in need of shelter; we want successful placements and adoptions.

To God be the Glory. Ase

Acknowledgments
EPILOGUE

SPIRIT LED APPROACH
TO
PARENTING

Healing brokenness in the Family Structure

To much is given, much is required

No one can step into the next level without support, encouragement, and friends who are committed to the friendship no matter what. This book birthed out of pain that I endured from the loss of my child, Joy. My vision, passion, and commitment to continue helping children strive for excellence. My deep gratitude to my friend, Sheldon Bailey from New Orleans who critiqued me and my work in love. While continuously encouraging me day after day. My sincerest thanks to you. Finally, my gratitude flows from heart to my daughter Iiesha Ernestine Balkcom and my grandchildren, Mia Simone, Martin William and Ivy J. Latonia. Thank you for loving me unconditionally. My journey continues.